BEVERLY HILLS PUBLIC LIBRARY

3 5048 00490 1276

D1616769

WITHDRAWN

CREATIVE EDUCATION

J
796.962
Goodman

MIGHTY DUCKS

M I C H A E L E. G O O D M A N

BEVERLY HILLS PUBLIC LIBRARY
444 N. REXFORD DRIVE
BEVERLY HILLS, CA 90210

Published by Creative Education
123 South Broad Street, Mankato, Minnesota 56001
Creative Education is an imprint of The Creative Company

Designed by Rita Marshall
Cover Illustration by Rob Day

Photos by: Bruce Bennett Studios and Wide World Photos

Copyright © 1996 Creative Education.
International copyrights reserved in all countries.
No part of this book may be reproduced in any form without written
permission from the publisher.
Printed in the United States of America.

Library of Congress Cataloging-in-Publication Data

Goodman, Michael E.
Anaheim Mighty Ducks / Michael E. Goodman.
p. cm. — (NHL Today)
ISBN 0-88682-746-9

1. Anaheim Mighty Ducks (Hockey team)—History—Juvenile literature.
[1. Anaheim Mighty Ducks (Hockey team)—History. 2. Hockey—History.]
I. Title. II. Series.

GV848.A53G66   1995   94-46768
796.962'63'0979496—dc20

23456

A SPECIAL BRAND OF ENTERTAINMENT

On October 19, 1993, the Mighty Ducks of Anaheim faced off against the New York Rangers for the first road game in their history. Most hockey experts thought the game was a mismatch. After all, the Rangers were favored to contend for the Stanley Cup during the 1993–94 season. The expansion Ducks, on the other hand, with their strange name and connection with the Walt Disney Company, were expected to play comically and end up near the bottom of the Pacific Division of the National Hockey League (NHL).

Terry Yake was with the team from the beginning.

Sean Hill scored the team's first-ever goal in their opening game on October 8, 1993.

The crowd in New York's Madison Square Garden acted hostile toward the Ducks, not like the friendly fans in California. They shouted insults, held up pictures of Mickey Mouse, and even quacked sarcastically.

But the jeering seemed to spur on the Ducks. With less than eight minutes remaining in the game, Anaheim led 3-2 and was threatening again on a power play. The Ducks' No. 1 line of Troy Loney, Anatoli Semenov, and Terry Yake was on the ice. Yake had already scored two of Anaheim's first three goals and was hoping to earn a place in team history by recording its first hat trick ever. The short-handed Rangers readied to defend their goal. Defenseman Sean Hill got the puck to Semenov, who moved in on New York goaltender Mike Richter. Semenov spotted Yake off to his right and made a perfect pass. A split-second later the puck was in the Rangers net. Yake had his hat trick, the Ducks were on their way to winning their first game on the road, and the New York fans stopped laughing at the Mighty Ducks of Anaheim.

The Mighty Ducks surprised a lot of hockey fans during their first NHL season, tying the record for most wins by an expansion team and setting a new mark for most road wins by a first-year club. Despite their youth and inexperience, the Ducks certainly didn't play like a new team. They instantly established a rivalry with their Southern California neighbors, the Los Angeles Kings, and won over an audience of both children and adults for their special brand of entertainment on the ice.

Anatoli Semenov was one of the Ducks' top scorers (page 7).

Ron Wilson led the new team to 33 wins, tying the Florida Panthers for an NHL record.

It is not surprising that the city of Anaheim gave the Mighty Ducks such a warm welcome when they arrived on the scene in 1993. Anaheim residents have a long history of welcoming newcomers. The first settlers in the area were the Gabrielino and Juaneno Indians. They were joined in the 1600s and 1700s by Spanish missionaries and ranchers. Then, in the middle of the nineteenth century, a group of German farmers purchased blocks of land along the Santa Ana River at two dollars per acre. They named their new settlement Anaheim, which in German meant "home by the Ana River." The farmers planted grapes and began making wine. When a blight wiped out the grape vineyards in the 1880s, the farmers successfully turned to cultivating oranges.

Anaheim remained a small, quiet place until 1955, when cartoonist and entertainment pioneer Walt Disney opened Disneyland there. Suddenly, the boom was on. Over the next 38 years, Anaheim's population increased nearly 900 percent—from 30,000 in 1955 to more than 266,000 in 1993. And that is not counting the millions of visitors who came to the area each year to visit Mickey Mouse and his friends.

When the Mighty Ducks joined the boom, they became the third professional sports team to find a home in the Southern California city. Previously, the California Angels baseball club and Los Angeles Rams football franchise had moved the 28 miles southeast from Los Angeles to Anaheim. But the Ducks were different from the other two teams. Their franchise was the first to begin in Anaheim, rather than be transplanted there, and it was the only one to proudly incorporate the name of the city in its own name.

Before the Mighty Ducks became a reality in Anaheim, they were an idea in the mind of Michael Eisner, the chairman of the Walt Disney Company. It took a special imagination, like Eisner's, to think of bringing a new ice hockey team to sunny Southern California.

Eisner grew up in New York City, where he was an avid NHL fan. He passed along that love of hockey to his three sons, and all of them played in youth hockey leagues in Los Angeles. At 6:00 many winter mornings, Eisner and his wife Jane would be in the stands watching their sons compete on the ice.

A few years later, in the early 1990s, the city of Anaheim began building a large marble-and-glass arena two miles from Disney-land. The city leaders did not have a definite plan in mind about how to use the arena. However, as Eisner drove by the building site every morning on his way to work, he began to formulate his own ideas. Eisner was already involved in a hockey project at the time. He had convinced the movie production division at Disney to develop a comedy about a group of misfit youngsters who were brought together to form a winning youth hockey team, the "Mighty Ducks." The movie was a big success, and Eisner began imagining a grown-up Mighty Ducks hockey squad playing in the new Anaheim arena.

Several obstacles stood in Eisner's way, however. For one thing, Bruce McNall, the owner of the Los Angeles Kings, had exclusive rights to professional hockey in the Los Angeles metropolitan area. Eisner would have to get McNall's permission and probably need to pay a hefty fee to start a new franchise so close to Los Angeles. Eisner was also not so sure that buying a pro-

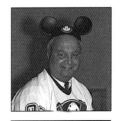

With an eye for talent, Jack Ferreira, the Ducks' first general manager, put together a successful team.

Guy Hebert was Anaheim's top pick in 1993 (pages 10-11).

fessional hockey team would be a good investment for his company. He hired an independent consultant to study the idea, and the consultant reported back favorably.

Soon afterward, Eisner worked out an agreement with McNall to waive the Kings' territorial rights for a $25 million fee. Then Disney and Ogden Entertainment Services, managers of the new Anaheim arena, formed a partnership to establish an NHL franchise in Anaheim starting in the 1993–94 season. They also gave the arena a new name—"The Pond" —because young hockey players traditionally compete on frozen ponds. (The building's official name is the Arrowhead Pond of Anaheim.)

The next question was what to call the team. Eisner had a fast answer: "The Mighty Ducks." That didn't go over so well with some of the NHL leaders at first. "Someone from the league called

Joe Sacco was the only player to appear in all 84 games of the inaugural season.

and tried to talk me out of it," Eisner recalled. "But I said, 'Look, you can tell me anything you want about hockey, but marketing is an area we know about at Disney.'"

Eisner began marketing the new team right away. First he asked Disney artists to help design a unique logo for the club, and more than 200 employees submitted entries. The design that was picked features a goalie's mask shaped to fit a duck's head over crossed hockey sticks. The duck's expression seems playful and sinister at the same time. The colors chosen for team jerseys were also unusual—purple and jade. The new team name, logo and colors caught on right away with kids in Southern California and all around the United States. Long before the Mighty Ducks were ready to play their first hockey game, millions of American youngsters were wearing team jerseys, caps and T-shirts printed with catchy mottos such as "These Ducks Shoot Back!"

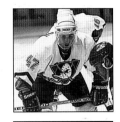

Stephan Lebeau joined the Ducks mid-season and added ten points in 22 games.

THE FIRST TEAM

The Ducks' owners knew that no matter how great the marketing, the new franchise would be a success only if the team performed well on the ice. Jack Ferreira, a man with more than 20 years of experience running hockey teams, was hired as the club's first general manager. Ferreira's main task would be to put together a competitive club from two different sources — a pool of NHL players (mostly aging veterans or inexperienced young players) who were left unprotected by their current teams and a draft of amateur and minor league players who had no NHL experience. Ferreira felt confident that enough talent would be available from the two groups to form a solid nucleus for the new hockey team.

Bobby Dollas played in his 200th NHL game on December 22, 1993.

In two pressure-packed days, June 25-26, 1993, Ferreira picked 35 players for the club. He had a clear plan in mind. The Anaheim general manager believed that the Ducks' first priorities should be goaltending and defense. He wanted to build a team that could hold down opponents' offense rather than one that tried to out-skate and outscore the opposition. The club's offensive attack could be developed over time, Ferreira said, but defense was an immediate need, particularly in a division that included such offensive powerhouses as the Los Angeles Kings, Vancouver Canucks and Edmonton Oilers. Following this plan, Ferreira used several of his early picks in the expansion draft to choose goaltender Guy Hebert from the St. Louis Blues and defensemen Alexei Kasatonov from the New Jersey Devils, Sean Hill from the Montreal Canadiens and Bill Houlder from the Buffalo Sabres. In later rounds, Ferreira selected two additional veteran back-liners, Bobby Dollas and Randy Ladouceur, who would become the backbone of the Anaheim defense in the club's first year.

While he focused on veterans for defense, Ferreira looked to acquire quick, young skaters to play the center and wing positions on the club. His forward selections in the expansion draft included Steven King, Tim Sweeney, Terry Yake, Bob Corkum and Joe Sacco—all under 27 years of age. In addition, Ferreira's first pick in the NHL entry draft for players who had no previous NHL experience was 18-year-old forward Paul Kariya from the University of Maine, the top college player in America in 1993.

Ferreira's next problem was to find a coach with the patience and experience to handle an expansion team. He interviewed several candidates and then offered the job to 38-year-old Ron Wilson, who had served as assistant coach of the Vancouver

Steven King had the longest home goal-scoring streak (page 15).

Randy Ladouceur,
with 823 career NHL
games, had the most
NHL experience of
any Anaheim
player.

Canucks since 1990. Wilson was not well known to most hockey experts, but he was young, energetic and upbeat—all of which appealed to Ferreira. Wilson also had a solid hockey background. He had played for seven years in the NHL before becoming a coach, and both his father and uncle were NHL veterans. In addition, with his experience in Vancouver, Wilson already knew a lot about the other Pacific Division clubs.

Wilson came on board on June 30, and got to work right away. He knew he had only 10 weeks to mold a group of mismatched players into a cohesive team before the October 8 season opener. That task would challenge even a Disney hero.

Alexei Kasatonov was the oldest player the first season.

Bobby Dollas was
acquired from
Detroit in the 1993
NHL Expansion
Draft.

Throughout August and September of 1993, excitement began to build in Anaheim as the Mighty Ducks prepared for their first NHL game against the Detroit Red Wings on October 8 at The Pond. Every available ticket was sold weeks before the game, and a standing-room-only crowd of 17,300 fans packed into the building on opening night to cheer on their new heroes.

The starting lineup for the Ducks featured Guy Hebert in goal, Alexei Kasatonov and Randy Ladouceur on defense, Anatoli Semenov at center, and Troy Loney and Terry Yake on the wings. The Anaheim players skated nervously around the face-off circle. They were psyched up for this historic night—maybe a little too much. The stronger, faster Red Wings got off to a quick start, peppering Hebert in goal with 20 shots in the first period

alone. Hebert made one outstanding stop after another, but his acrobatics weren't enough. At 2:34 of the first period, Detroit's Aaron Ward put his club up 1-0, and the barrage was on. By game's end, the Red Wings had scored an easy 7-2 victory, sending the Anaheim fans home unhappy. They did have one real moment of excitement, however, early in the second period when Sean Hill scored the Ducks' first goal ever on a power play. It was a night of many firsts for Hill. He also recorded the team's first shot and committed the Ducks' first penalty.

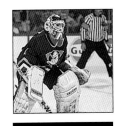

Ron Tugnutt set a club record for most saves (46) in a single game.

The Anaheim players trooped into their locker room after the game with their heads down. But coach Wilson wouldn't let them stay depressed for long. He told the players that one reason for the bad loss was that the team had lost its defensive focus in all the excitement. The New York Islanders would be at The Pond two nights later, he added, and that would be a chance to turn things around right away.

A SUCCESSFUL FIRST SEASON

The Ducks made sure they were ready for the Islanders, and the second game of the season turned out to be one of the most exciting of the year. With under a minute to go in the tight defensive struggle, the Islanders were up 3-2. Coach Wilson took goalie Ron Tugnutt out of the game for a sixth skater. The Ducks closed in on the New York net, tying the contest on Bob Corkum's goal with only 31 seconds to go to send the game into overtime. Anaheim eventually lost the contest, but they learned an important lesson: if they concentrated hard on defense, they could be competitive against almost any team in the league.

The Ducks proved that point even more dramatically over the

In 1993-94, Bill Houlder was the top-scoring defenseman.

next 10 days. They captured their first victory ever with a 4-3 triumph over Edmonton at the Pond on October 13, tied contests against Boston and Calgary a few days later, and began their first road trip successfully with their "mighty" win over the New York Rangers that featured Terry Yake's hat trick. Remarkably, the Ducks' record stood at 2-2-2 after their first six games.

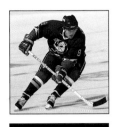

Tim Sweeney scored a career-high 43 points in the team's first season.

Unfortunately, the club could not keep up its winning ways. Anaheim lost its next four road games and its first two contests after returning home. But nearly every game was close; there were no more blowouts as on opening night. Like any expansion team, the Ducks were inconsistent, but they were slowly coming together. During the rest of the season, they experienced only one bad losing streak and played extremely well on the road. Their final record away from The Pond was 19-20-3, the best ever by an expansion club. With an overall record of 33-46-5, the Ducks finished the year with 71 points. That put them in fourth place in their six-team division. Even more important, the Mighty Ducks won the "Battle of Los Angeles" in their first year in the league, finishing ahead of the fifth-place Kings.

"I never once went into a game that year thinking we didn't have a chance to win, and I know the players didn't either," recalled general manager Jack Ferreira as he looked back on the team's first season.

The 1993-94 season was also a success financially for the Mighty Ducks ownership. The Pond was sold out for 27 of its 41 home games, and an average of over 16,000 cheering fans attended each home game. The Pond quickly earned a reputation as one of the noisiest arenas in the league, especially when a Ducks player scored a goal. That's when thousands of fans would begin tooting

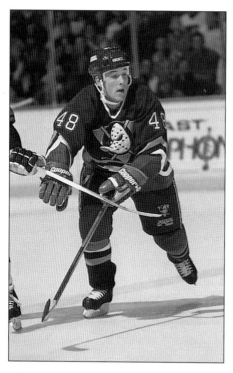

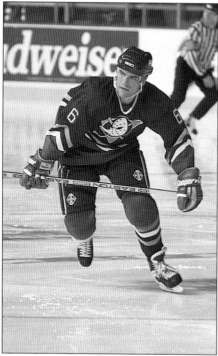

Left to right: John Lilley, Patrik Carnback, Sean Hill, Stephan Lebeau.

on duck calls sold at the arena concession stands. It often sounded like hunting season in The Pond when a Mighty Duck lit the red goal light.

Several new NHL standouts emerged during the Ducks' inaugural year. The club's top goal scorer was center Bob Corkum, who tallied 23 times, despite usually having to play against the opposition's best defenders. Anaheim's overall scoring leader was Terry Yake with 52 points. Both young men had been buried on the benches of their old NHL teams in 1992-93, but they proved they could shine for the Ducks when they were given an opportunity to play. Top goaltender Guy Hebert also had an excellent year, allowing less than three goals per game in 52 appearances and stopping more than 90 percent of opposition shots on his net. On the defensive side, Bobby Dollas and Randy Ladouceur not only led the way on the ice but also provided important veteran leadership. Bill Houlder was the team's best backline scorer, totaling 14 goals and 25 assists.

Tom Kurvers was a top playmaker, leading the team in power play assists (21).

LOOKING AHEAD

Anaheim finished its first season on a particularly strong note, winning eight of its last 14 contests, and the team optimistically looked ahead to its second year in the league.

"We're solid in goal and have some good role players in place as a nucleus," Coach Wilson noted during the off-season. He added that the club had still had two major needs to fill, however—a fast-skating center and a dominant defenseman.

Ferreira potentially solved one of those problems when he signed defenseman Oleg Tverdovsky, a powerful 18-year-old defenseman from Russia, to play in Anaheim. Tverdovsky was

Bob Corkum led the team in goal-scoring (pages 26-27).

28   *Paul Kariya played most of the 1993-94 season preparing for the 1994 Olympics.*

the Ducks' first draft pick in 1994 and second pick overall in the draft.

"When I saw Tverdovsky play in Russia, he brought me out of my seat," Ferreira commented. "Down the line, he'll be the man who'll run our power play—the offensive defenseman every championship team has. I think he has the ability to be a star."

Tverdovsky will solidify the team's defense, its strongest area, but the Ducks still need to build a more explosive offensive attack in order to rise in the league standings. Wilson and Ferreira proved in 1993–94 that they were both patient and savvy when it came to developing a solid hockey team in Anaheim, and their players showed that they were willing to work hard. It may take a few more years, but the club plans to fly high in the NHL.

Shaun Van Allen tallied 33 points his first full season in the NHL.

Patrik Carnback finished his rookie season with 23 points.

Steve Rucchin was Anaheim's second pick in the 1994 Supplemental Draft.   31

Anaheim Mighty Ducks
Buffalo Sabres
Boston Bruins
Calgary Flames
Chicago Blackhawks
Dallas Stars
Detroit Red Wings
Edmonton Oilers
Florida Panthers
Hartford Whalers
Los Angeles Kings
Montreal Canadiens
New Jersey Devils
New York Islanders
New York Rangers
Ottawa Senators
Pittsburgh Penguins
Philadelphia Flyers
St. Louis Blues
San Jose Sharks
Tampa Bay Lightning
Toronto Maple Leafs
Vancouver Canucks
Washington Capitals
Winnipeg Jets